CARNATIC CAFE

Dr. Priya Mohan

notionpress
.com

INDIA · SINGAPORE · MALAYSIA

Copyright © Dr. Priya Mohan 2024
All Rights Reserved.

ISBN 979-8-89415-229-5

Synopsis

The famous quote "Art never dies" applies to cooking as well. A lot of authentic recipies are in oblivion, due to a lack of timely documentation. This cook book, is one such ensemble collection, of the choicest of recipes, from various people, whom I have admired for their exceptional culinary skills. It also reflects my personal relationship with food and how I would like to prepare it.

Sounds trite, but I cannot help mentioning my mother as my greatest inspiration for more unusual reasons than the ordinary. She gave me a free hand to experiment in her kitchen, has intervened only when necessary and let me learn from my mistakes. That said, she has also bailed me out of many culinary disasters, quite adroitly, with her practical tips and sound advice. My sister, Maya, is instrumental in giving my culinary skills that magical twist, with her constant encouragement and support, as I dared to experiment with different cooking styles with lively trepidation.

Thanks, both of you, for also helping me marshal the content for this gastronomic adventure!

This book is not only designed for the competent cook but also serves a healthy dose of inspiration for the confident and expert cooks. Providing new insights, it revisits and puts a new spin on traditional South Indian cuisine.

This handy manual is devoid of the usual "cheffy" jargon and relies solely on simplicity and clarity for its appeal and traction. It is a modest attempt to connect with readers through a shared love of healthy, home cooked fare. Despite lacking the bandwidth of a comprehensive cook book, this compilation targets a fairly overlooked aspect of time management, which is an important need of the hour today. Planning and organization are more time consuming than actually whipping up a dish.

The objective of this cooking guide, is to take care of that lacuna, saving mental energy through a standard structured protocol for each dish. The idea of limiting it to 44 recipies is that one dish can be tried everyday of the month. If it were a large book, most of the recipies will not be tried and will remain as recipies in the book instead of translating into tasty dishes.

The most important ingredients to add to your cooking, irrespective of the recipe are love, positive vibes, focus and passion; the phenomenal impact of these can definitely be perceived by whoever is eating it.

My interest in culinary affairs embarked early on... I still remember the fried rice I made in my seventh grade. It was during this interesting journey I realised one thing...that true essence of cooking was neither a matter of ballastic adjustments of ingredients nor an outcome of tried and tested traditional recipes

The most important ingredient to be infused are love and passion- that makes all the difference

This cookbook is a compilation of a few recipes I learnt thus far from various teachers to whom I am eternally grateful- mother,grandmothers,aunts, neighbors,friends and online cooking channels to name a few.

I also dedicate this cookbook to my late grandfather, Mr A.N. Subramanyam, who was a connoisseur of good food. He has played a pivotal role in giving direction to my culinary skills.

The most important ingredient to be infused are love and passion- that makes all the difference

Contents

SWEETS

1. Javvarisi Payasam (Sabudana Kheer) 7
2. Manga Pachadi 8
3. Pineapple Kesari 9
4. Semiya Payasam (Vermicelli Kheer) 10

UPMA

5. Javvarisi (Sabudana) Upma 12
6. Vegetable Semiya Upma 13
7. Rava Upma 14
8. Vegetable Poha Upma 15

PONGAL

9. Semba Ravai Pongal (Wheat Pongal) 17
10. Sweet (Chakkarai) Pongal 18
11. Ven Pongal 19

IDLI AND DOSA

12. Idlis 21
13. Semolina Snack 22
14. Artisan Adai 23
15. Dosa Recipe 24

RICE

16. Bisibela Bath 26
17. Jeera Rice-Pressure Cooker 28
18. Lemon Rice 29
19. Methi (Fenugreek) Rice 30
20. Pudina (Mint) Rice 31
21. Thayir Sadham (Curd Rice) 32
22. Tomato Rice 33
23. Vegetable Brinji 34

SAMBAR

24. Aviyal 36
25. Dal Fry (with garlic) 37
26. Keerai Kootu 38
27. Mixed Vegetable Kurma 39
28. More Kuzhambu 40
29. Sambar Powder/Sambar Podi 41
30. Sambar 42
31. Vegetable Poricha Kootu 44

RASAM

32. Lemon Rasam 46
33. Milagu Rasam 47
34. Paruppu Rasam 48
35. Rasam Powder/Rasam Podi 49

CURRY

36. Baingan Ka Bhartha 51
37. Beans Poriyal 52
38. Paruppu Usilli 53
39. Potato Saagu 54

CHUTNEY

40. Coconut Chutney 56
41. Curry Leaves Thogayal 57
42. Onion Tomato Chutney 58
43. Thayir Pachadi 59
44. Thengai (Coconut) Thogayal 60

SWEETS

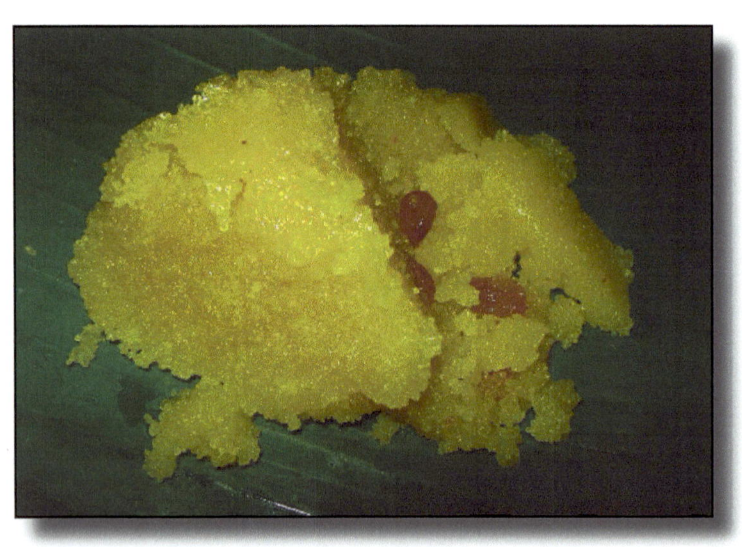

Javvarisi Payasam (Sabudana Kheer)

INGREDIENTS

- ½ cup of Sago well soaked for ½ an hour
- 3 cups of standardised milk
- 1 ¼ cups of sugar
- ¼ tbsp cardamom powder
- ¼ tbsp nutmeg
- 4–5 saffron strands
- 10 cashews
- 10 Raisins
- 1 tbsp Ghee
- 2 cups Water

MAKING JAVVARISI PAYASAM

- Wash the sago well and soak in water for 20 minutes at least.
- Cook it on a low to medium flame in 1½ cups to 2 cups of water, stirring occasionally, (to avoid burning of sago grains) till it becomes soft and transparent.
- Take out a pellet and examine it properly before proceeding further.
- Boil the milk and then add to the cooked sago, stirring on and off, on a low to medium flame, then add the sugar and stir very well.
- Now add the saffron strands, cardamom and nutmeg powders.
- In a pan add ghee and fry the cashews till golden brown and raisins until they're plumped up. Drop them into the payasam for that final finishing touch.

Some people like me like it hot, while there are quite a few who like it chilled. Either way, this dulcet delight is 'straight fire'.

This saccharine delight is my all-time favourite! Javvarisi payasam means 'sago sentiment', in my dictionary, for a valid reason. In the hostel, where I stayed during my undergraduate days this 'blockbuster' would be served on several memorable occasions. Even now, partaking of this delectable dish at home or in a function triggers 'sweet' memories of my college days!

Sago is a coolant during hot summer days and is a soothing demulcent for an irritated stomach.

Manga Pachadi

This is a traditional sweet made on Tamil New Year's Day. This pachadi is packed with the 6 flavours-salt, sweet, spice, bitter, sour and astringent.

INGREDIENTS

- 2 raw mangoes, peeled and cut into small chunks
- ½ cup jaggery, powdered
- ¼ teaspoon Turmeric powder
- 1 green chilli,slit
- ½ teaspoon salt

TEMPERING

- ½ teaspoon mustard seeds
- 1 tsp urad dal
- 1 sprig curry leaves
- 2 dry red chillies, broken into half
- 1 tablespoon oil

MAKING MANGA PACHADI

1. Pare the raw mango and cut into small chunks.
2. Add the raw mango into the pressure cooker, along with salt, turmeric powder.
3. Add ½ cup of water and pressure cook for 3 whistles and turn off the heat.
4. Allow the pressure to release naturally.
5. Open the cooker and add the powdered jaggery. Stir and cook on a low flame for a couple of minutes.
6. Heat oil in a pan over medium heat; add the mustard seeds, urad dal, and red chillies. Stir until the seeds crackle.
7. Add the curry leaves and finally stir in the cooked pachadi.
8. Bring it to one brisk boil and turn off the heat.
9. Serve the Pacha Manga Pachadi along with steamed rice, chappathi, or upmas.

Pineapple Kesari

INGREDIENTS

- 1 cup Semolina/Rava
- 1½ cups fresh ripe pineapple
- 2 cups Sugar
- 3 cups Water
- ½ cup ghee
- Salt – A pinch
- 4–5 Saffron threads
- ¼ tsp cardamom powder
- ¼ tsp nutmeg powder
- 10 Cashew nuts- split into halves
- 10–12 dried raisins
- 2 drops yellow food colour

MAKING THE KESARI

1. Dice the pineapple, avoiding the central portion. Chop the pineapple into fine pieces. Sprinkle 3 tablespoon of sugar and keep aside for 30 mins.

2. Heat a kadai. Add a tablespoon of ghee and roast the cashews and raisins till cashews are golden brown and raisins plump. Transfer to a plate.

3. In the same kadai, add a tablespoon of ghee and fry aromatic on a medium flame. Keep aside on a plate.

4. Again, in the same kadai, add 1 tablespoon of ghee and saute the pineapple pieces for a couple of minutes on a low flame.

5. To this add water and boil, adding a pinch of salt and the saffron strands till the colour is uniformly distributed.

6. Now add the roasted rava, stirring continuously to avoid the formation of lumps.

7. Add the sugar and stir so that the sugar blends with the rava and pineapple mixture well.

8. Now add the cardamom and nutmeg powders, the remaining ghee, stir well.

9. Finally add the raisins, and cashew nuts.

10. Cover with a lid and cook on low flame for a couple of minutes.

11. Once the kesari is thick, switch off the flame. Add little ghee on top.

12. Serve Hot!

Semiya Payasam (Vermicelli Kheer)

INGREDIENTS

- 500 ml Standardised Milk
- 1/2 cup Semiya (Vermicelli), roasted
- 1 cup Water
- ½ cup Sugar
- 3 tablespoons cashewnuts, halved
- 3 tablespoons raisins
- ¼ teaspoon cardamom powder
- 2-3 saffron strands
- 1 tablespoon ghee

MAKING SEMIYA PAYASAM

1. Into a heavy bottomed pan, add the water and the semiya and bring to a boil. Once the semiya begins to boil, turn the heat to medium and cook the semiya until it is soft and done. Drain the excess water into another bowl.

2. Once done, add the 500 ml of milk, sugar, cardamom powder and saffron and stir until the sugar dissolves completely.

3. Simmer the payasam for another 5 minutes till the flavors are absorbed well and the payasam looks thick and creamy.

4. You can adjust the consistency of the payasam, based on your preference.

5. In a small pan, heat ghee on low heat; add in the cashew nuts and roast until crisp and golden. Add in the raisins, stir for a few seconds until it puffs up and keep aside.

6. Turn off the heat and finally garnish the Semiya Payasam with the roasted cashew nuts and raisins and serve the payasam hot or cold as desired.

Note: The semiya payasam on cooling down, thickens. You can adjust the thickness with the water drained from cooking the semiya.

UPMA

Javvarisi (Sabudana) Upma

INGREDIENTS

- 1 cup javvarisi
- Water to soak
- ½ cup peanuts
- ½ cup cubed potatoes
- 1 medium onion finely chopped
- 2 green chillies finely chopped
- Salt to taste
- 2 tbsps of finely chopped coriander for garnishing
- 1 tsp sugar

TEMPERING

- 2 tbsps oil
- 1 tsp cumin seeds (jeera)
- 2 green chillies chopped fine
- 2 tsps channa dal
- 1 tsps urad dal (split)
- 1 tsp mustard seeds
- Curry leaves (few leaves)

MAKING THE UPMA

1. Soak javvarisi in water for about 2 hours.

2. Drain completely and keep it aside overnight.

3. Roast the peanuts and crush coarsely. Mix the javvarisi with salt, sugar and half of the coarsely ground peanuts. Keep aside.

4. Heat the oil in a kadai. Add in mustard seeds. When it sputters, add in the urad dal and channa dal. Once golden brown, add the jeera and curry leaves.

5. Next add the finely chopped onions, green chillies and saute till the onions turn pink and translucent.

6. Add the javvarisi and cook over a low flame, keeping the kadai covered for 3 to 4 minutes.

7. Stir the upma, checking to see if the javvarisi is well cooked.

8. Sprinkle the coriander leaves leaves and the remaining roasted peanuts.

9. Serve hot with chutney, preferably a sweet chutney.

Vegetable Semiya Upma

INGREDIENTS

- 1 cup semiya (roasted vermicelli)
- 1 small onion finely chopped
- 1 green chilli finely chopped
- 1 tsp ginger –grated
- Salt to taste
- 1 and 1/2 cups water (hot)
- 2 tbsps of finely chopped coriander for garnishing
- 1 tsp Lemon juice (optional)

TEMPERING

- 2 tbsps ghee
- 2 tbsps oil
- 1 dried red chilli (Kashmir Chillies/Byadagi/ Guntur)
- 2 tsps channa dal
- 1 tsps urad dal (split)
- 1 tsp mustard seeds
- A pinch of asafoetida
- Curry leaves (few leaves)

VEGETABLES (1 CUP)

- 1 medium Carrot finely chopped
- 5 beans chopped
- ½ cup peas
- A few cauliflower bits

MAKING THE SEMIYA UPMA

1. Heat the oil in a kadai. Add in mustard seeds. When it sputters, add in the urad dal and channa dal. Once golden brown, add the asafoetida and curry leaves.

2. Next add the finely chopped onions, green chillies and grated ginger and saute till the onions turn pink and translucent.

3. Add the chopped vegetables to the kadai and saute for a few minutes.

4. Cook on a low flame. Check that the vegetables are partially cooked.

5. Pour water and add salt to the kadai. Bring the water to a boil.

6. Add the vermicelli to the water and keep tossng it in the kadai till the water is absorbed. Depending on the type of vermicelli, you may need more water. Add little by little.

7. Reduce the flame and cook covered for a couple of minutes.

8. Turn off the flame and fluff the upma, adding a teaspoon of ghee. *At this stage, lemon juice can be added. However, this is optional.*

9. Serve hot with chutney.

Rava Upma

INGREDIENTS

- 1 cup rava/Suji/semolina
- 1 medium onion finely chopped
- 2 green chillies finely chopped
- 1 tsp ginger -grated
- Salt to taste
- 2 cups water (hot)
- 2 tbsps of finely chopped coriander for garnishing
- 1 tsp Lemon juice (optional)

TEMPERING

- 2 tbsps ghee
- 2 tbsps oil
- 1 dried red chilli (Kashmir Chillies/ Byadagi/Guntur)
- 2 tsps channa dal
- 1 tsps urad dal (split)
- 1 tsp mustard seeds
- A pinch of asafoetida
- Curry leaves (few leaves)

MAKING THE UPMA

1. Heat the oil in a kadai. Add in mustard seeds. When it sputters, add in the urad dal and channa dal, Once golden brown, add the asafoetida and curry leaves.

2. Next add the finely chopped onions, green chillies and grated ginger and saute till the onions turn pink and translucent.

3. Add the rava and keep tossng it in the kadai for 1-2 minutes. A spoon of ghee at this point will enhance the taste of the upma.

4. Reduce the flame and pour 2 cups of hot water, little by little, stirring all the while.

5. The suji will thicken. Sprinkle the coriander leaves leaves and cover the kadai with a lid. Simmer for 5 minutes.

6. Turn off the flame and fluff the upma, adding a teaspoon of ghee. *At this stage, lemon juice can be added. However, this is optional.*

7. Serve hot with chutney.

Vegetable Poha Upma

INGREDIENTS

- 2 cups Pohan (flattened rice-aval)
- Salt to taste
- ½ tsp Turmeric Powder
- 2 tbsps Lemon juice
- 1 onion finely chopped
- 2 green chillies finely chopped
- 1 tsp ginger grated
- 1 carrot chopped fine
- 6 Beans- chopped fine
- 1 Potato peeled and chopped into small chunks
- ¼ cup water

TEMPERING

- 2 tbsp ghee /2 tbsps oil
- 1 tsp urad dal (split)
- 1 tsp mustard seeds
- A pinch of asafoetida
- A sprig of curry leaves

INSTRUCTIONS

1. Take the poha in a colander and add water. Squeeze out the water.

2. Add salt, turmeric and lemon juice and set it aside.

3. Heat oil/ghee in a pan and add mustard seeds, urad dal and asafoetida till the mustard seeds sizzle.

4. Add in onions, green chillies, ginger and sauté for a minute.

5. Add the chopped vegetables, salt and turmeric and mix well. Cook till vegges are cooked.

6. Add poha and cook, mixing the vegetables well with the poha.

7. Serve hot with chutney.

PONGAL

Semba Ravai Pongal (Wheat Pongal)

INGREDIENTS

- 1 cup rice
- 3 tbsps moong dal (pasi paruppu)
- Ghee 2 tsps
- Salt to taste
- Water

TEMPERING

- 1 tbsp ghee
- 1 teaspoon cumin seeds (jeera)
- 1½ teaspoon black pepper corn coarsely ground
- 1 inch ginger peeled and chopped finely
- 2 Green chillies finely chopped
- A pinch of asafoetida
- Curry leaves (few leaves)
- 10 cashew nuts

MAKING THE WHEAT RAVA PONGAL IN PRESSURE COOKER

1. Heat the pressure cooker. Add ghee and temper with pepper, cumin, green chillies, curry leaves and asafoetida. Saute I medium flame for 30 seconds.

2. Roast the moong dal and add the wheat rava and stir.

3. Add salt, and about 4 cups of water.

4. Pressure cook for 3 whistles in medium flame.

5. When the pressure releases naturally, open the lid. Mash the wheat rava and dal so that it is mushy. If the consistency seems too dry, add boiling water, and cook on low flame.

6. Heat 2 tablespoons of ghee In a pan. Fry the split cashew nuts till golden brown.

7. Serve hot with chutney or sambar.

Sweet (Chakkarai) Pongal

INGREDIENTS

- ½ cup rice
- ¼ cup moong dal (pasi paruppu)
- 3 cups of water
- 10 cashew nuts
- 2 caradamom (yellakai)
- 10 raisins
- ¾ cup jaggery (vellam)
- 1/3 cup of water
- Pinch of camphor (edible) or 5 strands of saffron
- 2 tablespoons ghee

MAKING THE SWEET PONGAL USING PRESSURE COOKER

1. Roast the moong dal on a low flame in a pressure cooker.
2. Add the rice to the roasted dal.
3. Rinse the rice dal mixture and add it to pressure cooker.
4. Pour 3 cups of water to the rice dal mixture.
5. Pressure cook for 5 whistles on a medium flame.
6. When the pressure releases naturally, open the lid. Mash the rice and dal so that it is mushy. If the consistency seems too dry, add boiling water, and cook on low flame.
7. Add the water to jaggery and heat it till the jaggery melts completely. Keep stirring all the while.
8. Strain the jaggery syrup and keep aside.
9. Add the jaggery syrup to the rice dal mix in the pressure cooker.
10. Add ghee to the mixture and cook in low flame.
11. Add cardamom powder and camphor/saffron
12. Heat 2 tablespoons of ghee in a pan. Fry the split cashew nuts till golden brown. Add to Pongal mix.
13. Enjoy Chakkarai Pongal!

Ven Pongal

INGREDIENTS

- ½ cup rice
- ½ cup moong dal (pasi paruppu)
- 3 to 3½ cups of water
- 1 tsp ginger –grated
- Salt to taste

TEMPERING

- 2 tbsps ghee
- 10 cashew nuts
- ¾ teaspoon cumin seeds (jeera)
- ½ teaspoon black pepper corn coarsely ground
- 1 inch ginger peeled and chopped finely
- A pinch of asafoetida
- Curry leaves (few leaves)

MAKING THE VEN PONGAL COOKER AND SALT TO TASTE.

1. Roast the moong dal on a low flame in a pressure cooker.

2. Add the rice to the roasted dal.

3. Pour 3 to 3 ½ cups of water to the rice dal mixture.

4. Add salt to taste. Stir well.

5. Cook for 2 whistles on a medium flame.

6. When the pressure releases naturally, open the lid. Mash the rice and dal so that it is mushy. If the consistency seems too dry, add boiling water, and cook on low flame.

7. Heat 2 tablespoons of ghee In a pan. Fry the split cashew nuts till golden brown. Keep aside.

8. Next, in the same pan add jeera, pepper. When it splutters add the ginger, asafoetida and curry leaves.

9. Add this to the cooked Pongal. Mix well and let it simmer for a few minutes on a low flame.

10. Serve hot with chutney or sambar.

IDLI
and
DOSA

Idlis

INGREDIENTS

- 1/2 cup Urad Dal
- 1 1/2 cups Rice Rava
- ½ tsp fenugreek seeds
- 1 teaspoon rock salt
- 2 table spoons Poha
- Water to grind rice

INSTRUCTIONS (IDLI BATTER- USING A BLENDER)

1. Wash the urad dal and fenugreek seeds in water and soak it for over 6 hours.
2. Wash the idli rava and soak in water for 6 hours.
3. Rinse and soak poha 20 minutes before blending in mixie.

METHOD FOR MAKING THE IDLI BATTER

1. Drain the water from both the soaked bowls of urad dal and feugreek as well as idli rava.
2. Blend the urad dal and fenugreek seeds, soaked and drained poha,salt and water with a little water (2 to 3 tablespoons).

3. Squeeze the soaked Rava by hand and add it to the ground Dal.
4. Blend all them well and keep aside for 8-10 hours in a large utensil with a lid.
5. The idli batter will ferment to nearly doubling in volume in 6 hours.

MAKING THE IDLIS

1. Boil water in an Idli steamer or pressure cooker on a medium flame.
2. Grease the Idli plates with oil.
3. Mix the idli batter a couple of times gently.
4. Fill the greased moulds with the batter and place in the idli steamer.
5. Steam for 8 to 10 minutes.
6. Remove the idli stand and let it cool. A toothpick/fork should could come out clean when inserted in the idli.
7. Remove the idlis gently with a spoon and serve with idli milagai podi/chutney or sambar.

RAVA IDLY

Popular in karnataka, rava idli is a semolina based tiffin item, served with saagu and chutney. Nothing recondite about it, once you master the actual technique. Rava idlies are lower in calories and are therefore a healthy breakfast option. The following recipe is a lucid, uncomplicated version and perhaps the only recipe you may follow henceforth. It is designed by a retired military cook, with an arsenal of culinary skills, who toiled endlessly in the army kitchens.

INGREDIENTS

- Semolina or Bombay Rava 1 cup
- Ghee 2 Tbsp
- Mustard Seeds ½ Tsp
- Cumin Seeds ¼ Tsp
- Channa Dal ½ Tsp
- Cashew Chopped 1 Tbsp
- Asafoetida a pinch
- Curry Leaves a sprig
- Green Chillies 2 slit
- Ginger grated 1 Tbsp
- Salt 1/2 Tbsp
- Coriander Leaf 2 Tbsp
- Curd 1 cup
- Water 1/3 cup
- Lemon Juice 1 Tsp
- Cooking Soda 1/4 Tsp
- Cooking Oil or Ghee 1 Tbsp
- Optional Grated carrot, capsicum, Boiled Peas- 1 Tbsp

METHOD

1. Heat 2 tbsp ghee in a thick bottomed pan fry the cashews till light golden brown set aside.

2. Thereafter, to the same pan, add the mustard, cumin, asafoetida, and once they splutter add the channa dal till, it riddled a bit add the crushed curry leaves, green chillies ginger and quickly fry on a low to medium flames till aromatic (i.e. for 20 secs).

3. Then add the rava mix well roast over a low flame until the rava turns fragrant and brittle (but not brown)

4. Set aside to collect completely even if the rava used is already pre-roasted, it is better to roast it lightly once again.

5. Then add salt, coriander leaves, curd and 1/3 cup water mix well to get a batter of smooth, uniform consistency. Cover this set aside for ½ hours (30 mins).

6. Grease the idly plates with oil or ghee and sprinkle the grated carrots, capsicum, boiled peas and position a roasted cashew in the center of each mould.

7. Mean while bring the water to a rolling boil in an idli cooker or pressure pan.

8. Examine the consistency of the batter, which should be like regular idly batter, neither too thick not too thin.

9. Add fresh lemon juice, mix well and then add the baking soda whisk gently in only one direction and briskly transferred to the mould in idly plates.

10. Place the preheated pressure pan or idly cooker and steam for 10-12 mins on a high flame.

11. Once cool, insert a fork into the rava idly to check whether it is done (come out clean with very little crumbs.

12. Carefully remove the idlis from the mould once cool with a wet spoon or butter knife.

13. Serve hot with coconut or tomato chutney or sambar.

Artisan Adai

ADAI

This easy to make, lentil pancake, is chock full of nutrients, recommend by most dieticians for healthy weight loss. Popular in Tamil Nadu and Kerala, adai is partaken with aviyal, butter, jaggery, idly podi or chutney. Drumstick leaves can be added to bolster it's nutritional value. Adai dosai and pesarattu are similar equivalents, worth a mention. The following 'artisan' adai recipe is an abridged innovation of the several variations that exist. Do check out, sometime!

INGREDIENTS

- 1 Cup Rice (Parboiled or Idly Rice)
- ¼ Cup Channa Dal
- ¼ Cup Toor Dal
- 1/8 Cup Moong Dal
- 1 Tbsp Urad Dal
- 1/8 Cup Sago
- 1 Tbsp Grated Ginger
- 5 Byadige Red Chillies
- ½ Tsp Jeera
- ¼ Tsp Asafoetida
- Salt As required
- Enough water to make Batter
- 3 Tbsp Cooking Oil
- 4-5 Shallots or Spring Onion
- Curry leaves- Chopped
- 1 Tbsp Coriander Leaves- Finely chopped

OPTIONAL INGREDIENTS

- Drumstick leaves- 1 cup
- Grated carrot- ½ cup
- TIME
- Preparation time: 10 minutes
- Soak time: 2-4 hrs
- Cook time: 25 minutes
- Serve: 10 adais

PREPARATION

1. I find it convenient to soak the rice, Dals, sago and red chillies together for 2-3 hours for crispy adais. For adaidosai, an overnight soak of upto 8 hours may be approximate (in which case rice and dal can be soaked separately).

2. Completely drain the water and first add the red chillies, then the rice and lentils.

3. Thereafter add the grated ginger and asafoetida, cumin and green chillies.

4. Grind to a coarse batter in pulse mode, then add ½-¾ cup water, in instalments and grind to a semi coarse batter.

5. Empty the batter into a mixing bowl, cover and allow it to ferment for 1hour at least.

6. Now add the finely chopped shallots or spring onions coriander curry leaves, grated carrot and drumstick leaves.

7. Add salt and blend well. I personally prefer thinner adais, so the batter I prepared is not very thick.

8. Smear a decent amount oil on a heavy tawa and let it heat up well.

9. Pour a ladle full of batter on the hot tawa and quickly spread out the batter in a circular.

10. Drizzle some oil over the corners, cook on low to medium flame till adai is crisp and golden flip it over till Cooked well on both sides. Flip again and serve hot with aviyal, jaggery, white butter chutney or idly podi.

Dosa Recipe

INGREDIENTS

- 1/2 cup Urad Dal
- 1 1/2 cups Raw rice
- ½ tsp fenugreek seeds
- 1/2 teaspoon rock salt
- 2 table spoons Poha
- Water to grind rice and dal

INSTRUCTIONS (DOSA BATTER- USING A BLENDER)

1. Wash the urad dal and fenugreek seeds in water and soak it for over 6 hours.
2. Wash the rice and soak in water for 6 hours.
3. Rinse and soak poha 20 minutes before blending the batter.

METHOD FOR MAKING THE BATTER

1. Drain the water from both the soaked bowls of urad dal and fenugreek as well as rice., adding the rock salt.
2. Blend the urad dal and fenugreek seeds, and soaked poha with a little water. The batter should be of a thick pouring consistency. Pour into a large utensil and keep aside.
3. Next blend the drained rice, adding a little water to get a thick pouring consistency.

4. Transfer this into the vessel with the batter and mix well, adding the rock salt.
5. Cover the vessel and leave to ferment.

MAKING THE DOSA

1. Place the tawa on the gas and heat to medium.
2. Grease the with oil using a cut onion to prevent the dosa from sticking to tawa.
3. Sprinkle a few drops of water on tawa. If it sizzles, the tawa is ready.
4. Lower the heat of the tawa, a pour a ladle of dosa batter on the hot tawa.
5. Spread it evenly starting from centre outwards.
6. Drizzle oil round the edges of the dosa, slowing raising the heat to high.
7. Once the dosa is crisp, turn it round using a spatula, moving slowly from the edges inwards.
8. Cook the other side for 30 seconds or so.
9. Fold the dosa and serve hot with chutney and sambar.

FOR MASALA DOSA

For the potato filling, sauté mustard seeds, curry leaves, onions, and boiled, diced potatoes in oil. Spread the batter on a hot tava, place the potato filling, fold the dosa, and cook until crispy.

RICE

Bisibela Bath

INGREDIENTS

For the bisibela bath

- ¾ cups rice (I use Paccha Ponni rice)
- ½ cup tuvar dal (thoram paruppu)
- Small lemon sized ball of tamarind
- 2 tablespoons ghee or oil
- Salt to taste
- ¼ tsp turmeric
- A small lump of jaggery

TEMPERING

- 1 tablespoon ghee
- 1 spring of curry leaves
- 10 cashews split
- Pinch of asafoetida
- 1 tsp mustard seeds
- 1 red chilli broken (Guntur, Kashmir or Byagadi)

VEGETABLES

- 1 cup of assorted vegetables dice (carrots,peas,beans,potatoes,capsicum)
- 1 medium onion finely chopped/4 shallots (chinna vengayam)

BISI BELA BATH POWDER

- 1 inch cinnamon
- 1 bay leaf (tej patta)
- 3 cloves
- 1 tsp cumin (jeera)
- 1 tsp urad dal
- 1 tsp channa dal
- ¼ tsp fenugreek seed (methi)
- 1 ½ tbsp coriander seeds (dhaniya)
- 1 marathi moggu
- A little dessicated coconut

BISIBELA BATH POWDER

- Dry roast red chillies, channa dal and urad dal till you get the aroma of the dals. Transfer to a plate.
- Next roast the coriander seeds, cloves, cinnamom and maratha moggu. Transfer again to the plate.
- Roast the methi seeds and cumin on a low flame.
- Cool the roasted ingredients.
- Powder along with the dessicated coconut and keep aside.

MAKING THE BISIBELA BATH IN PRESSURE COOKER

1. Wash the rice and dal well.
2. Pour 2 ¾ water in the pressure cooker and add the rice and dal to it. Add a little salt and turmeric to it. The total salt must be spread over the rice,dal and vegetables evenly.
3. Pressure cook for 3 to 4 whistles. Let it cool naturally. The rice dal mixture must be mushy.
4. Soak the tamarind in hot water. Squeeze it and filter into a bowl.
5. Heat a pan with 1 tsp of ghee.
6. Saute the cut vegetables alongwith the shallots in the pan for a few minutes.
7. Add 1 cup of water to the vegetables and cook till nearly done. Add a little salt to the vegetables while cooking in water.
8. Pour the tamarind from the bowl to the pan with vegetables. Let it boil for a couple of minutes.
9. Now add the mashed rice dal mix to the pan adding 1 cup of water to the mixture.

10. The rice dal mix must come to a boil on a medium flame.

11. Add the Bisibela Bath Powder with a little jaggery to the rice-dal-vegetables-tamarind mix in the pan and stir well till the desired consistency is reached.

12. On cooling the Bisibela bath will become hard, so stop heating when the consistency is slightly watery.

13. Temper the Bisibela bath with mustard seeds, curry leaves and asafoetida.

14. A generous dollop of ghee with every serving along with papad will be a great meal.

Jeera Rice-Pressure Cooker

INGREDIENTS

- 1 ½ cup basmati rice
- 2 tablespoons ghee or oil
- 1 green chilli slit
- 2 ½ cups of water
- Salt to taste
- Coriander leaves for garnishing

SPICES

- 2 teaspoon cumin seeds (jeera)
- 1 bay leaf (tej patta)
- 4 cardamoms (Yellakai)
- 2 inch cinnamom piece (pattai)
- 4 cloves (lavangam)

MAKING THE JEERA RICE IN PRESSURE COOKER

1. Wash the rice well. Soak in water and let it stand for 20 minutes.

2. Heat the pressure cooker. Add ghee and saute bay leaf, cinnamon, cardomoms until they begin to sizzle.

3. Next, add the jeera to the pressure cooker and roast on low flame till you can smell the aroma.

4. Add the slit green chilli.

5. Drain the basmati rice and add to the pressure cooker. Gently fry it, without breaking the rice grains.

6. Add salt, and about 2 ½ cups of water and stir well.

7. Pressure cook for 2 whistles on a high heat.

8. When the pressure releases naturally, open the lid. Fluff the jeera rice with a fork. Garnish with coriander leaves.

9. Serve hot with curry or dal.

Lemon Rice

INGREDIENTS

- 1 ½ cup rice (basmati, raw rice)
- 1 medium sized lemon
- 2 tablespoons ghee or oil
- ¾ teaspoon mustard seeds
- 2 tablespoons peanuts
- ¼ tsp turmeric
- 2 green chillies chopped fined
- ½ tablespoon ginger chopped fine
- 2 red chillies (Kashmir/Guntur/Byadagi)
- 1 spring curry leaves
- 1 ½ tsp channa dal
- 1 tsp urad dal
- A pinch of asafoetida
- 2 ½ cups of water
- Salt to taste
- Coriander leaves for garnishing

MAKING THE LEMON RICE

1. Wash the rice well. Soak in water and let it stand for 20 minutes.

2. Cook rice in the pressure cooker as usual. (*For 1 cup of rice I use 1 ¼ water while using a pressure cooker. However, the variety of rice used will make a difference. So please use your discretion!*).

3. On cooling, open the pressure cooker and fluff up the rice.

4. Spread it on to a wide plate so that though the rice is fully cooked, it is not mushy.

5. Heat a pan with ½ tablespoon oil/ghee on a medium flame.

6. Add the peanuts and fry till golden. Transfer the peanuts to a plate.

7. Next add the remaining oil/ghee to the pan. Add mustard seeds, urad dal and channa dal and red chillies.

8. Now add the ginger, green chillies, curry leaves, and asafoetida, turmeric and salt.

9. Switch off the stove.

10. Add the cooled rice to the pan.

11. Take two spatulas and mix uniformly so that the rice is infused with the fried mixture.

12. Squeeze the lemon juice on the mixed rice and once again stir well.

13. Garnish with roasted peanuts and coriander leaves.

14. Serve with curd, appalam or pickle.

Methi (Fenugreek) Rice

INGREDIENTS

- 1 cup cooked basmati rice
- 1 ½ cups of methi leaves
- ¾ cup chopped onions
- 2 green chillies
- ¾ tbsp ginger garlic paste
- 1 tablespoons ghee
- 2 tbsp refined oil
- Salt

SPICES

- 1 bay leaf (tej patta)
- 4 cardamoms (Yellakai)
- 1inch cinnamom piece (pattai)
- 2 cloves (lavangam)
- ½ tsp cumin seeds

MAKING THE METHI RICE

1. Wash the rice well. Soak in water and let it stand for 20 minutes.
2. Wash the methi leaves in a colander thoroughly.
3. Heat the pressure cooker. Add ghee and saute bay leaf, cinnamon, cardomoms,cloves and cumin seeds till they crackle.
4. Next sauté the chopped onions till translucent. Then add the green chilli, ginger garlic paste. Sauté till the raw aroma dissipates.
5. Now add the methi leaves to the pan and saute for 2 mnutes till cooked.
6. Add the cooked rice with salt and stir.
7. Use a spatula to mix well without breaking the rice grains.
8. Serve hot with curd and papad.

Pudina (Mint) Rice

INGREDIENTS

- 1 ½ cups rice (I use Paccha Ponni or Basmati rice)
- 2 ½ cups water for pressure cooker
- 2 tablespoons oil
- Salt to taste
- 1 cup pudina (mint)
- 2 green chillies
- 1 tablespoon ginger grated
- 3 garlic pods
- 1 medium onion finely chopped
- Coriander leaves, finely chopped, for garnishing
- 1 tablespoon lemon juice

SPICES

- 2 inch cinnamon
- 1 bay leaf (tej patta)
- 1 star anise
- 4 cardamom pods
- 6 cloves
- ¾ teaspoon cumin seeds (jeera)

MAKING THE PUDINA RICE IN PRESSURE COOKER

1. Wash the rice well. Soak in water and let it stand for 20 minutes.
2. Wash the mint leaves and drain them. Coriander leaves can also be mixed if liked.
3. Grind mint, green chillies, ginger, garlic, chopped onion to a smooth paste.
4. Heat the pressure cooker. Add 2 tablespoons oil and saute bay leaf, cinnamon, cardamoms, star anise, cumin and clove until they begin to sizzle.
5. Next, add the ground paste to the pressure cooker and saute on low flame till you can smell the aroma.
6. Pour the water into the pressure cooker and bring to a boil. Add salt and stir well.
7. Add the drained rice and stir well till the mixture blends.
8. Close the pressure cooker and cook for 2 whistles on medium flame.
9. Let the pressure cook stand and cool naturally.
10. Open the lid and stir gently. Pour lemon juice and mix well.
11. Serve hot with kurma or pachadi.

Thayir Sadham (Curd Rice)

INGREDIENTS

- ½ cup rice
- 1 ½ cups water
- 1 ½ cups curd
- ½ cup boiled milk
- Salt

SPICES

- 1 ½ tsp oil
- ½ tsp mustard seeds
- ½ tsp jeera
- Pinch of asafoetida
- 1 sprig curry leaves
- ¾ tbsp channa dal
- ½ tbsp urad dal
- 2 Red chillies (Guntur/Kashmir)

MAKING THE CURD RICE

1. Wash the rice well. Soak in water and let it stand for 20 minutes.
2. Cook the rice in a pressure cooker with 1 ½ cups water for 2 whistles. Allow to cool naturally.
3. Open the pressure cooker and mash the rice while it is hot.
4. To the mashed rice add the boiled milk and stir.
5. Let this mixture cool.
6. On cooling add the salt and curd. Again mix well.
7. Fry mustard and cumin, urad dal and channa dal in a little oil.
8. To this add curry leaves, broken red chillies and asafoetida.
9. Pour this over the curd rice.
10. Decorate with pomegranate seeds.

Tomato Rice

INGREDIENTS

- 1 ½ cups rice (I use Paccha Ponni or Basmati rice)
- 2 tablespoons ghee or oil
- 1 medium onion finely chopped
- 1 green chilli slit
- 1 tablespoon ginger garlic paste
- 1 cup tomatoes finely chopped
- ¾ teaspoon salt
- 1 teaspoon garam masala
- ½ teaspoon chilli powder
- ½ teaspoon turmeric
- 2 ½ cups water for pressure cooker
- Coriander leaves, finely chopped, for garnishing
- 1 tablespoon lemon juice

SPICES

- 1 inch cinnamon
- 1 bay leaf (tej patta)
- 2 cardamom pods
- 3 cloves
- ¾ teaspoon cumin seeds (jeera)

TO GARNISH

- 2 teaspoon oil
- 4-5 cashews
- 1 slice bread

MAKING THE TOMATO RICE IN PRESSURE COOKER

1. Wash the rice well. Soak in water and let it stand for 20 minutes.

2. Heat the pressure cooker. Add 2 tablespoons oil and saute bay leaf, cinnamon, cardomoms cumin and clove until they begin to sizzle.

3. Next, add the onions, ginger garlic paste, green chilli, to the pressure cooker and saute on low flame till you can smell the aroma.

4. Add the cut tomatoes,salt and ¼ tsp turmeric.

5. Saute for 3-4 minutes till the tomatoes infuse the aromas of the spices and turn mushy.

6. Add ½ tsp chilli powder and ¾ tsp garam masala powder. Mix well and keep sauteing till tomatoes are well blended. The tomato masala mixture should leave the sides of the cooker.

7. Pour the water into the pressure cooker and bring to a boil. Add salt and stir well.

8. Add the drained rice and stir well till the mixture blends.

9. Close the pressure cooker and cook for 2 whistles on medium flame.

10. Let the pressure cook stand and cool naturally.

11. In a pan, add ghee and fry the cashews separately.

12. Garnish with cashews and finely chopped coriander.

13. Serve hot with curry or dal.

Vegetable Brinji

INGREDIENTS

- 1 cup rice (I use Paccha Ponni)
- 2 cups of finely chopped assorted vegetables (carrots,beans,peas,potatoes)
- 2 tablespoons ghee or oil
- 1 cup coconut milk
- ¾ cup water1 tsp salt
- 1 tbsps oil + 1 tbsp ghee
- 1 inch cinnamon
- 1 bay leaf (tej patta)
- 2 cardamom pods
- 2 cloves
- 1 medium sized onion finely chopped
- 1 tsp crushed garlic
- Salt to taste
- Coriander leaves for garnishing

TO GARNISH

- 2 teaspoon oil
- 4-5 cashews
- 1 slice bread

MAKING THE BRINJI RICE IN PRESSURE COOKER

1. Wash the rice well. Soak in water and let it stand for 20 minutes.
2. Heat the pressure cooker. Add oil and saute bay leaf, cinnamon, cardomoms and clove until they begin to sizzle.
3. Next, add the onions, ginger, garlic,chillies to the pressure cooker and saute on low flame till you can smell the aroma.
4. Add the mint leaves and mix well.
5. Add the vegetables and saute for 3-4 minutes till the vegetables infuse the aromas of the spices and mint.
6. Add the coconut milk, water and salt to the pressure cook and stir well. and let the mixture cook in medium flame for a couple of minutes.
7. Add the drained rice and stir well till the mixture blends.
8. Close the pressure cooker and cook for 2 whistles on medium flame.
9. Let the pressure cook stand and cool naturally.
10. In a pan, add ghee and fry the cashews and bread pieces separately.
11. Add to the cooked brnji.
12. Garnish with coriander and serve.
13. Serve hot with curry or dal.

SAMBAR

Aviyal

INGREDIENTS

- 1 cup thick curd
- ¼ tsp turmeric
- 2 cups of assorted vegetables: cut length-wise in julienne style
  - Drumsticks
  - Carrots
  - Raw plaintain
  - Pumpkin
  - Ash gourd
  - Green beans
  - Yam
  - Snake gourd
- ½ of a coconut, freshly broken and grated
- Salt to taste
- 1 tsp cumin seeds (jeera)
- 4 green chillies
- A blob of jaggery
- 3 tablespoon-Coconut oil
- Curry leaves for garnishing

MAKING AVIYAL

1. Cook the cut vegetables in a thick bottomed pan with about ¾ to 1 cup of water.
2. Grind the coconut, green chillies and cumin to a fine paste adding a little water.
3. Whisk the curd with salt and turmeric powder.
4. Mix the ground paste in the whisked curd.
5. Add the cooked vegetables to the curd
6. Mix gently. Add jaggery. Simmer the aviyal for a minute and switch off the heat.
7. Add 3 tbsps coconut oil to the avial.
8. Garnish with curry leaves.
9. Close with a lid and let the flavours blend.
10. Serve with hot rice along with an appalam.

Dal Fry (with garlic)

INGREDIENTS

- 1 cup tuvar dal
- ¼ cup moong dal
- 2 cups of water
- 1 medium size onion
- 1/3 cup finely chopped tomatoes
- 2 green chillies split
- 2 dried red chillies
- A sprig of Curry leaves
- 1 inch ginger grated
- 4 cloves of garlic
- 1 tsp mustard seeds
- 1 tsp urad dal
- T tsp cumin seeds
- A pinch of asafoetida
- ½ tsp turmeric powder
- ¼ tbsp red chilli powder
- 2-3 tbsp ghee
- 2 tbsp oil
- 2 tbsp lemon juice
- Coriander leaves for garnishing
- Salt as required
- Water to adjust consistency

MAKING DAL FRY

1. Soak the dals in 2 cups of boiling water for 15 minutes in a pressure cooker.

2. Add a pinch of turmeric and 1 tbsp oil and pressure cook the dals on medium flame for 8 to 9 whistles.

3. Open the pressure cooker when cool and mash the dal well, using a hand blender or ladle.

4. Heat 1 tbsp ghee in a a thick bottomed pan. Add the mustard seeds, followed by urad dal, cumin seeds and dried red chilli.

5. Now add the chopped onions and fry till translucent.

6. Add the crushed garlic and ginger and sauté till the raw aroma disappears.

7. Add the green chillies, red chilli powder, asafoetida and sauté further, lowering the flame to sim.

8. Now add the tomatoes and keep stirring will the they are mushy and the oil seeps from the side.

9. To the mushy tomatoes add the cooked dal, salt and a little water, stirring consistently over a low flame. Once the dal is smooth and creamy turn off the stove.

10. Garnish with coriander leaves.

11. Serve hot with steamed rice, brinji, chappatis or pooris.

Keerai Kootu

INGREDIENTS

- 1/2 cup yellow moong dal
- 2 bunches of palak (*Note: Depends on the size of the bunch!*)
- 1/2 cup cubed tomato optional
- 1/4 tsp turmeric powder
- Salt to taste

GRIND WITH WATER TO A SMOOTH PASTE:

- 2 tbsps grated coconut
- 1 red chilli
- ½ tsp jeera
- 2 shallots (chinna vengayam)

TEMPERING

- 1 tsp oil
- 1 tsp mustard seeds
- 1 tsp urad dal
- 1 red chilli broken into halves (Kashmir or Guntur)
- A spring of curry leaves

MAKING KEERAI KOOTU

1. Wash the spinach several times and chop it.
2. Cook the moong dal with a pinch of turmeric in a pressure cooker for 3 whistles. Let it cool naturally.
3. Open the pressure cooker and mash the dal well.
4. Heat a thick bottomed pan and cook the spinach with a little turmeric. Add about ¼ cup of water.
5. When the spinach is cooked add the mashed moong dal to it. Add a little water and salt and mix well.
6. Grind the grated coconut, red chilli, shallots, jeera and pepper to a fine paste.
7. Add the ground paste to the mashed dal and vegetables. Stir well.
8. Heat in medium flame for a few minutes till well blended.
9. Temper the kootu with mustard seeds, urad dal and red chilli.
10. Garnish with curry leaves. This can be eaten with rice or as a side dish.

Mixed Vegetable Kurma

INGREDIENTS

- Kurma Paste
- ¼ cup of coconut
- 12 to 15 cashews – soaked
- 2 teaspoons poppy seeds (khus khus)
- ½ tablespoon roasted chana dal (roasted split & husked bengal gram)
- ½ tablespoon coriander seeds
- 1 teaspoon fennel seeds
- ½ teaspoon cumin seeds
- 3 cloves
- 2 green cardamoms
- 4 to 5 black peppercorns
- 1 kapok bud (marathi moggu)
- ½ piece stone flower
- 2 green chilies
- 1 ½ tsp ginger garlic paste
- ½ cup water for blending or add as required

VEGETABLES

- ¾ cup cups cauliflower florets (medium sized)
- 1 cup chopped potatoes – diced
- ½ cup green peas
- ¼ cup french beans –chopped
- ¼ cup carrots–chopped

OTHER INGREDIENTS

- 2 tablespoons oil
- 1 medium sized onion finely chopped
- 1 medium tomato finely chopped
- 1 sprig curry leaves
- ¼ teaspoon turmeric powder
- ½ teaspoon red chili powder
- 2 tablespoons curd
- Water as required
- Salt to taste
- Coriander leaves for garnishing

MAKING MIXED VEGETABLE KURMA

1. Soak cashews and poppy seed in hot water for 10 mins and grind along with the rest of the ingredients mentioned for making kurma paste. with a little water to a semi coarse paste.

2. Heat a pressure cooker. Add 3 tbsp oil, sauté the whole spices (cinnamon, bay leaf, cardamom, cloves) till aromatic.

3. Add onion and sauté till translucent.

4. Then add the curry leaves and the tomato till soft and mushy and the oil seeps out.

5. Toss in the vegetables with 1 tsp salt and sauté for 3 minutes.

6. Add 2 cups water and pressure cook for 1 whistle. Open the cooker on cooling.

7. Add on the ground masala paste to the semi-cooked vegetables and stir for 2 to 3 minutes

8. Now add 1 ½ cups of water stir well, cook for 10 to 12 minutes till the vegetables are completely cooked.

9. Garnish with chopped coriander leaves serve hot with poori, chappathi, rice and oven idly.

More Kuzhambu

INGREDIENTS

- 1 cup thick curd
- ¼ tsp turmeric
- 2 cups of assorted vegetables: cut length-wise in julienne style

  Drumsticks

  Carrots

  Raw plaintain

  Pumpkin

  Ash gourd

  Green beans

  Yam

  Snake gourd
- ¼ of a coconut, freshly broken and grated
- Salt to taste
- 1 tsp tuvar dal + 1 tsp channa dal, soaked in ¼ cup water
- 1 tsp cumin seeds (jeera)
- 2 green chillies
- A blob of jaggery
- 1 tablespoon -Coconut oil
- Curry leaves for garnishing

TEMPERING

- 1 tsp mustard seeds
- 2 red chillies (Guntur/Kashmir/bygada)
- A pinch of asafoetida

MAKING AVIAYAL

1. Cook the cut vegetablesin a thick bottomed pan with about ¾ to 1 cup of water.
2. Grind the coconut, soaked dals, green chillies and cumin to a fine paste adding a little water.
3. Whisk the curd with salt and turmeric powder.
4. Mix the ground paste in the whisked curd.
5. Add the cooked vegetable to the curd
6. Mix gently. Add jaggery. Simmer the more kuzhambu for a minute and switch off the heat.
7. Temper the more kuzhambu with mustard seeds ,red chillies broken into bits, and asafoetida in 1 tablespoon coconut oil .
8. Garnish with curry leaves.
9. Close with a lid and let the flavours blend.
10. Serve with hot rice along with an appalam.

Sambar Powder/Sambar Podi

INGREDIENTS

- 4 tbsps coriander seeds (dhaniya)
- 1 tbsp tuvar dal
- 1 ½ tbsp channa dal
- 1 ½ tbsp urad dal
- ¾ tsps fenugreek seeds (methi)
- 2 tsp cumin (jeeraO
- 1 tsp peppercorn (milagu)
- 12 red chillies (Guntur/Byadagi/Kashmir)
- ¼ tsp of turmeric
- ½ tsp of asafoetida or a small lump of asafoetida
- A sprig of curry leaves

MAKING SAMBAR PODI

1. Clean all the ingredients.
2. Wipe the curry leaves with a wet cloth and dry them, either in the sun or in the microwave.
3. Heat a pan and roast the ingredients one by one, till you get the aroma of each item. Transfer to a plate. Let the flame be medium.
4. Ensure that the asafoetida is roasted well. The lump of asafoetida may sometimes be wet inside. So, keep tossing it in the pan till it is completely dry.
5. Lastly add the curry leaves and roast till crisp.
6. On the roasted ingredients cooling, powder in a grinder jar along with the turmeric.
7. Sambar powder should be stored in a clean dry jar.

Note: This sambar powder can be used to make a variety of sambars,like mullangi (radish) ,beans, brinjals, bottle gourd, drumsticks, pumpkin. The method is the same. Use 1 to 1 ½ tsp of sambar powder, depending on the quantity you make. Also cut vegetables appropriately, radish are cut as rounds; brinjals into quarters and so on.

Sambar

INGREDIENTS

- ¾ cup tuvar dal
- 2 cups water to cook dal
- 1 lemon size ball of tamarind soaked in 3 cups of water.
- 1 tsp jaggery
- Salt to taste
- ¼ tsp turmeric
- 1 ½ tsp sambar podi
- 2 tablespoons ghee or oil
- Coriander leaves for garnishing

VEGETABLES

- 12 shallots
- 1 large tomato
- 1 medium sized carrot diced
- 2 drumsticks cut into 2 inch pieces
- A small piece of pumpkin
- 1 green chilli slit

SAMBAR POWDER

Spices:

- 1 tablespoon coriander seeds
- 1 tablespoon chana dal
- 1 teaspoon urad dal
- ¼ tspn methi seeds
- 5-6 dried red chillies (Kashmiri or Byadagi)
- 1 tbsp jeera
- 1 tbsp peppercorn
- ¼ tsp of asafoetida powder or a bit of compounded asafoetida (LG Perungayam)

PREPARATION OF THE POWDER

- Heat a heavy bottom pan. Sauté each one of the spices individually and transfer to a plate. Allow the roasted ingredients to cool.
- Grind all the ingredients to a fine powder in a blender.
- Spread the sambar powder on a tissue paper and allow to cool.

TEMPERING

- 1 tablespoon ghee
- 1 spring curry leaves
- ½ teaspoon mustard seeds
- ¼ tsp methi seeds

MAKING THE SAMBAR

1. Wash the tuvar dal well.

2. Pressure cook the dal in 2 cups of water for 3 whistles.

3. Rinse the vegetables. Dice the vegetables to inch pieces. Shallots should be peeled and rinsed.

4. Drumsticks, 2inches a piece, should be cooked separately.

5. Heat a heavy bottomed pan. Add 1 tsp oil in the pan and saute the shallots for a minute. Then add all the diced vegetables one by one and saute for a couple of minutes.

6. Cook the vegetables and the green chilli till they are al dente. Add turmeric, sambar powder and salt to the vegetables.

7. The pulp of the tamarind soaking in water must now be extracted. Crush with your hands or a beater and strain the liquid to get a fairly thick extract.

8. Pour the tamarind extract over the vegetables and cook for 5 minutes.

9. Open the pressure cooker and mash the tuvar dal well with a masher.

10. Mix this into the sambar, stirring all the while. When the desired consistency is reached, add the jaggery. Stir well. Switch off flame.

11. Heat a small pan and temper the sambar in ghee curry leaves, mustard seeds and red chillies.

12. Add coriander leaves.

13. Serve hot with rice, idli, dosa and upma.

Vegetable Poricha Kootu

INGREDIENTS

- 1 carrot
- 1 potato
- 10 beans
- ½ cup of peas
- 1 drumstick
- ¼ cup moong dal
- ½ tsp turmeric
- Salt to taste
- 1 tsp peppercorns
- ½ tsp cumin seeds (jeera)
- 1 dried red chilli (Guntur/Kashmir/Byagada)
- 2 tbsps grated coconut

TEMPERING

- 1 tsp oil
- 1 tsp mustard seeds
- 1 tsp urad dal
- 1 red chilli broken into halves (Kashmir or Guntur)
- A spring of curry leaves

MAKING MILAGU RASAM

1. Wash the vegetables and chop them to cubes. The drumstick should be cut lengthwise -each 2 inches in length.

2. Cook the moong dal with a pinch of turmeric in a pressure cooker for 3 whistles. Let it cool naturally.

3. Open the pressure cooker and mash the dal well.

4. Heat a thick bottomed pan and cook the vegetables with a little turmeric powder. Cover the pan. (The drumstick can be cooked separately in another pan for about 5-6 minutes.)

5. When the vegetables are cooked add the mashed moong dal and mix well.

6. Add a little water and salt and mix well.

7. Grind the grated coconut, red chilli, jeera and pepper to a fine paste.

8. Add the ground paste to the mashed dal and vegetables. Stir well.

9. Heat in medium flame for a few minutes till well blended.

10. Temper the kootu with mustard seeds, urad dal and red chilli.

11. Garnish with curry leaves.

12. This can be eaten with rice and ghee or as a side dish instead of curry.

Note:

- *The masala can be ground after the coconut, red chilli, jeera and pepper are fried in oil.*

- *Pumpkin, snake gourd, cucumber can also be included in the kootu.*

RASAM

Lemon Rasam

INGREDIENTS

- 2 tablespoons moong dal
- 1 tomato chopped into quarters
- 2 cups water to cook dal
- Salt to taste
- ¼ tsp turmeric
- 1 ½ tsp rasam podi
- 1 tsp pepper cumin powder
- 2 tablespoons ghee or oil
- 1 lemon – squeezed (about 2 tbsps lemon juice)
- Coriander leaves for garnishing

TEMPERING

- 2 tsp ghee
- 1 tsp mustard seeds
- 1 red chilli broken into halves (Kashmir or Guntur)
- A spring of curry leaves

MAKING LEMON RASAM

1. Pressure cook the moong dal, slit green chill and turmeric in 2 cups of water for 3 whistles. Allow the pressure cooker to cool naturally.

2. Open the pressure cooker and mash the dal, chilli and turmeric. Add 2 cups of water.

3. Next add rasam powder, pepper cumin powder and salt.

4. Boil the rasam for about 5 minutes.

5. Add 1 cup of water to the rasam and reduce the flame to medium heat till a frothy layer is formed on the surface of the rasam.

6. Garnish with coriander leaves.

7. Heat a small pan and temper the rasam in ghee with curry leaves, mustard seeds and red chilli.

8. Add lemon juice and stir well.

9. Serve Lemon rasam with hot rice and curry or can be served in a cup as an appetiser.

Milagu Rasam (Pepper Rasam)

INGREDIENTS

- 1 gooseberry sized tamarind soaked in 1½ cup of water
- 2 large tomatoes chopped finely
- 2 tsps peppercorns
- 1 tsp cumin seeds (jeera)
- 1 tbsp sesame oil (nalla yennai)/sunflower oil/groundnut oil
- ¼ tsp turmeric
- 1 pinch of asafoetida
- 1 tsp rasam podi
- Coriander leaves for garnishing

TEMPERING

- 2 tsp ghee
- 1 tsp mustard seeds
- ½ tsp cumin seeds
- 1 red chilli broken into halves (Kashmir or Guntur)
- A spring of curry leaves

MAKING MILAGU RASAM

1. Extract the juice from the soaked tamarind. You must have at least 1 ½ cups of extract. Squeeze the tamarind pulp, strain and keep aside.

2. Crush the peppercorn and jeera coarsely and keep aside.

3. Heat oil in a heavy bottomed pan. Add mustard seeds first. After they crackle, add the dry chillies broken into bits and asafoetida. Saute till you get the aroma of the red chillies.

4. Next add the chopped tomatoes and curry leaves. Stir and saute on low heat till the tomatoes are mushy and soft.

5. Now add the turmeric and 1 tsp of rasam powder and saute further for a couple of minutes. Add the crushed peppercorn and jeera to the pan. Stir well.

6. Add the tamarind extract with about 2 cups of water. Add salt and stir.

7. Simmer on low flame for about 10 minutes. Once the rasam looks frothy on top, switch off the flame.

8. Close with a lid. Let the rasam stand and imbibe all the aromas of the varied spices.

9. Garnish with coriander leaves.

10. Serve with hot rice and ghee, along with an appalam or in a cup as an appetiser.

Paruppu Rasam

INGREDIENTS

- ½ cup of tuvar dal
- 1 gooseberry sized tamarind soaked in ½ cup of water
- 1 large tomato chopped into quarters
- 2 cups water to cook dal
- Salt to taste
- ¼ tsp turmeric
- 1 pinch of asafoetida
- 2 tsp rasam podi
- 2 tablespoons ghee or oil
- Coriander leaves for garnishing

TEMPERING

- 2 tsp ghee
- 1 tsp mustard seeds
- ½ tsp cumin seeds
- 1 red chilli broken into halves (Kashmir or Guntur)
- A spring of curry leaves

MAKING PARUPPU RASAM

1. Soak the tuvar dal for 10 minutes.

2. Pressure cook the tuvar dal and turmeric in 2 cups of water for 3 whistles. Allow the pressure cooker to cool naturally.

3. Open the pressure cooker and mash the dal, chilli and turmeric with a ladle.

4. Extract the juice from the soaked tamarind. You must have at least 1 ½ cups of extract.

5. Next add the chopped tomatoes, rasam powder, asafoetida and salt to the tamarind extract. Tamarind extract has reduced to about 3/4th its original volume. This may take about 10 minutes.

6. Add the mashed dal with 2 cups of water to the reduced tamarind extract and continue heating on a low flame.

7. Once the rasam looks frothy on top, switch off the flame.

8. Heat a small pan and temper the rasam in ghee with curry leaves, mustard seeds and red chilli.

9. Garnish with coriander leaves.

10. Serve with hot rice and ghee, along with a curry or in a cup as an appetiser.

Rasam Powder/Rasam Podi

INGREDIENTS

- ³⁄₄ cup coriander seeds (dhaniya)
- ¹⁄₄ cup tuvar dal
- ¹⁄₄ cup channa dal
- 2 tbsp cumin (jeeraO
- 2 tsps peppercorn (milagu)
- 6 red chillies (Guntur/Byadagi/Kashmir)
- ¹⁄₄ tsps fenugreek seeds (methi)
- 1 small lump of asafoetida
- 2 tsp rasam podi
- A sprig of curry leaves

MAKING RASAM PODI

1. Clean all the ingredients.
2. Wipe the curry leaves with a wet cloth and dry them, either in the sun or in the microwave.
3. Heat a pan and roast the ingredients one by one, till you get the aroma of each item. Transfer to a plate. Let the flame be medium.
4. Ensure that the asafoetida is roasted well. The lump of asafoetida may sometimes be wet inside. So, keep tossing it in the pan till it is completely dry.
5. Lastly add the curry leaves and roast till crisp.
6. On the roasted ingredients cooling, powder in a grinder jar.
7. Rasam powder should be stored in a clean dry jar.

CURRY

Baingan Ka Bhartha

INGREDIENTS

- 1 large purple eggplant (bhartha baingan or brinjal/aubergine)
- 2 tbsps refined oil
- 4-5 large garlic cloves
- 1 ½ inch ginger diced finely
- 1 green chilli finely chopped
- 1 large onion, thinly sliced
- 2 medium sized tomatoes chopped fine
- ½ tbsp red chilli powder
- 1 tbsp coriander powder
- Salt to taste
- 2 tbsp coriander leaves finely chopped

MAKING THE BAINGAN KA BHARTHA

1. Wash the eggplant well. Dry it with a clean cloth.
2. Smear oil all over it and plunge a skewer through it.
3. Roast it directly over a flame (of a stove) by placing it over the lighted stove.
4. Keep turning it around 10 to 12 minutes until all sides of it are completely roasted.
5. Test consistency by inserting a knife into the roasted eggplant. It should slide into the eggplant.
6. Duck the roasted eggplant into a bowl of water to cool.
7. Peel the skin and mash the pulp with a hand blender and set aside in a bowl.
8. Add oil to a heavy bottomed pan. Saute the garlic ginger and green chilli for 2 minutes.
9. Add the chopped onions cook till translucent.
10. Saute the chopped tomatoes to the onions and cook till the oil separates from the mixture..
11. Now add the mashed brinjal into the pan and mix well.
12. Season the bhartha with chilli powder and coriander powder and salt.
13. Mix well over a low medium heat stirring often for about 5 minutes.
14. Garniosh with coriander leaves.
15. Serve hot with roti, rice and ghee, or jeera rice.

Beans Poriyal

INGREDIENTS

- 2 tbsps oil
- 1 tsp mustard seeds
- ½ tsp asafetida
- 2 tsp urad dal
- ¼ tsp turmeric
- A sprig of curry leaves
- 1 dried red chilli
- 3 cups of French beans, trimmed and cut, ¼ inch pieces
- Salt to taste
- 2 cups water (hot)
- ¼ cup grated fresh coconut

MAKING THE PORIYAL

1. Heat the oil in a kadai. Add in mustard seeds. When it sputters, add in the urad dal and channa dal. Once golden brown, add the asafoetida and curry leaves.

2. Next add the chopped beans, salt, and turmeric. Sauté the beans for a minute.

3. Add 2 cups of water to the kadai. Cover and cook until the beans are tender.

4. Stir in the grated coconut.

5. Garnish with curry leaves.

6. Serve with Hot rice, ghee, sambar or rasam.

Note: This the basic poriyal (curry) recipe which we follow at home.

You can substitute carrots cubed into small pieces, Kothavarangar (cluster beans), kovakai, cabbage and other locally available vegetables. It is relatively fat free and easy to make.

Paruppu Usilli

INGREDIENTS

- 1 cup tuvar dal
- 4 dried red chillies
- ½ tsp asafoetida
- ½ tsp turmeric
- 1 tsp salt
- 1 tbsp oil
- 1 tsp mustard seeds
- 1 tsp urad dal
- A sprig of curry leaves

VEGETABLES

For Paruppu Usili you can use any of the following vegetables:

- French Beans (Beans)
- Cluster Beans (Kothavarangai)
- Broad Beans (Avarakkai)
- Cauliflower
- Banana Flower

MAKING THE PARUPPU USILI

- Soak the toor dal in water for about an hour.
- Drain fully using a colander.
- Add the tuvar dal, chillies, asfaoetida, and one tsp of oil and pulse in a blender. (Do no add water.)
- Add turmeric, salt and mix well.
- Take the idli cooker or a steamer. Grease the idli moulds and add little balls of the ground tuvar dal mixture to greased moulds.
- Steam for 6 minutes.
- Only cool, transfer the steamed usili to a plate and let it cool further.

MAKING THE PORIYAL

1. Take 2 cups of finely chopped vegetable (say beans) and cook in apressure cooker with a pinch of salt and turmeric. Switch off the cooker after 2 whistles.

2. On cooling, drain the beans and mix with the paruppu usili.

3. Heat the oil in a kadai. Add in mustard seeds. When it sputters, add in the urad dal and red chilli broken into bits. Once golden brown, add the asafoetida and curry leaves.

4. Next add the beans and usili mixture and cook it on a low flame for 2–3 minutes.

5. Serve with Hot rice, ghee, sambar or rasam.

Note: This the basic poriyal (curry) recipe which we follow at home.

You can substitute carrots cubed into small pieces, Kothavarangar (cluster beans), kovakai, cabbage and other locally available vegetables. It is relatively fat free and easy to make.

Potato Saagu

INGREDIENTS

- 1 ½ cups boiled potatoes, peeled
- 2 tbsps. oil
- 1 tsp mustard seeds
- 1 tsp urad dal
- 1 tbsp channa dal
- ¼ tsp turmeric
- 1 large onion, thinly sliced
- A sprig of curry leaves
- 2 green chillies, slit
- 1 tbsp grated ginger
- 1 tomato chopped fine
- A pinch of asafoetida
- 1 ½ tbsp besan (kadalai mavu)
- 1 ½ cups water
- Salt to taste
- 1 tbsp lemon juice
- 2 tbsps coriander leaves for garnishing

MAKING THE SAAGU

1. Heat the oil in a kadai. Add in mustard seeds. When it sputters, add in the urad dal and channa dal and sauté. Once golden brown, add the ginger, green chillies and curry leaves.

2. Add the thinly sliced onions and sauté until they are translucent.

3. Next add the chopped tomatoes and sauté for a few minutes till all ingredients are well blended.

4. Add the turmeric powder and asafoetida to the pan. Sauté and mix well.

5. Add the besan, sauté quickly and pour 1 ½ cups of water, giving the mixture a good stir.

6. Add the crumbled potatoes, and salt to the pan and mix well. Close the pan with a lid and cook over a low flame for 5 minutes. Test the consistency in between.

7. Switch off the flame, add lime juice and garnish with coriander leaves.

8. Serve hot with rava idly, dosa or poori..

Note: This the basic potato saagu (curry) recipe which we follow at home.

You can vary the consistency of the saagu according to your taste.

CHUTNEY

Coconut Chutney

INGREDIENTS

- ½ cup of grated coconut (Fresh newly broken coconut)
- 2 tablespoons of pottukadalai (fried gram dal)
- 2 green chillies
- Salt to taste
- 1 tsp lemon juice

TO TEMPER

- 2 teaspoon oil
- ½ teaspoon mustard seeds
- 1 teaspoon urad dal
- 1 sprig curry leaves

INSTRUCTIONS

1. Powder the pottu kadalai to a fine consistency.
2. Grind the grated coconut with the powdered pottu kadalai, green chillies and salt in a blender.
3. When the chutney is of the required consistency, transfer to a bowl.
4. Sauté the mustard seeds, urad dal and curry leaves in a kadai with oil and mix with the coconut chutney.
5. Add the lemon juice to the chutney and stir well.

Curry Leaves Thogayal

INGREDIENTS

- 4 cups fresh curry leaves tightly packed
- 1/2 cup grated coconut fresh
- 2 tsp oil
- 1 tsp mustard seeds
- 1 teaspoon urad dal
- 1/4 teaspoon hing asafoetida
- 4-5 dry red chillies
- A small piece of tamarind
- 1/2 cup chopped coriander leaves (optional)

INSTRUCTIONS

1. Wash the curry leaves thoroughly and set aside to drain
2. Heat oil in a pan and add the mustard seeds, followed by urad dal
3. When the dal turns brown, add the asafoetida.
4. Next add the red chillies.
5. Roast for 10 seconds and then add the curry leaves
6. Saute until the leaves wilt and turn a darker colour - about 5-7 minutes
7. Turn off the heat and add coconut, (coriander leaves), tamarind, and some salt
8. Stir everything together to warm up in the heat of the mixture
9. When cool grind with very little water to a coarse paste
10. Serve with rice and ghee

Onion Tomato Chutney

INGREDIENTS

- 2 small onions chopped into small cubes
- 2 small tomatoes sliced to small pieces
- 1 tsp red chilli powder, preferably Kashmiri Red Chilli powder.
- Salt to taste

TO TEMPER

- 2 teaspoon oil
- ½ teaspoon mustard seeds
- 1 teaspoon urad dal
- 1 sprig curry leaves

INSTRUCTIONS

1. Grind the onion and tomato to a fine paste without adding water.

2. Sauté the mustard seeds, urad dal ad curry leaves in a kadai with oil.

3. Add the ground paste to the kadai with the water, red chilli powder and salt.

4. Keep cooking the mixture on a medium flame, stirring all the while.

5. When the chutney reaches the desired consistency remove the kadai from the stove.

Thayir Pachadi

Thayir Pachadi is one of the traditional sides in any south Indian wedding or a function

INGREDIENTS

- 1½ cup Curd
- 1 teaspoon Oil
- ¼ teaspoon Mustard seeds
- A pinch Asafetida
- 3 tablespoon grated coconut
- 2 Green chillies
- ½ teaspoon grated ginger
- Salt to taste
- A sprig of curry leaves
- Coriander leaves for garnishing

TEMPERING

- ½ teaspoon mustard seeds
- 1 sprig curry leaves
- ¼ tsp asafoetida
- 1 tablespoon oil

MAKING THAYIR PACHADI

- Beat the curd with a whisk in a bowl.
- Grind the coconut, green chilies, and ginger to a smooth paste and add it to the beaten curd.   Add salt and mix well.
- Season the pachadi with mustard seeds, asafoetida, and curry leaves fried in oil.
- Mix well and garnish with coriander leaves finely diced.
- Serve fresh with rice dishes and chappathi.

Note: Variations of pachadi are chopping onions, cucumber and tomato and adding it to the whisked curd with salt and seasoning it.ns of thayir pachadi are

Thengai (Coconut) Thogayal

INGREDIENTS

- ½ tsp oil
- 3 tbsp urad dal
- 1 tsp mustard seeds
- One small lump of asafoetida
- 4 dried red chillies broken into halves (I prefer Byadagi, but Guntur and Kashmiri Chillies are great too!)
- 1 cup of grated freshly broken coconut.
- 1 tsp salt
- A small marble sized tamarind
- ½ cup water

INSTRUCTIONS

1. Soak the tamarind in a little water.
2. Heat oil in a pan and add the mustard seeds, followed by urad dal.
3. When the dal turns brown, add the asafoetida.
4. Next add the red chillies.
5. Mix it thoroughly. Roast for 30 to 45 seconds over medium heat.
6. Turn off the heat and add the coconut. Let this mixture cool.
7. Turn off the heat and add coconut, (coriander leaves), tamarind, and some salt
8. Thogayal is generally thick, so do not add too much water.
9. Store in an air tight container.
10. This can be eaten with hot rice and ghee.